INTRODUCING

Fascism
and
Nazism

Stuart Hood and Litza Jansz

Edited by Richard Appignanesi

ICON BOOKS UK   TOTEM BOOKS USA

This edition published in the UK in 2000 by Icon Books Ltd., Grange Road, Duxford, Cambridge CB2 4QF email: info@iconbooks.co.uk www.iconbooks.co.uk

Distributed in the UK, Europe, Canada, South Africa and Asia by the Penguin Group: Penguin Books Ltd., 27 Wrights Lane, London W8 5TZ

This edition published in Australia in 2000 by Allen & Unwin Pty. Ltd., PO Box 8500, 9 Atchison Street, St. Leonards NSW 2065

Previously published in the UK and Australia in 1993 under the title *Fascism for Beginners*

This edition published in the United States in 2001 by Totem Books

In the United States, distributed to the trade by National Book Network Inc., 4720 Boston Way, Lanham, Maryland 20706

Previously published in the United States in 1994 under the title *Introducing Fascism*

Library of Congress catalog card number applied for

ISBN 1 84046 154 3

Originating editor: Richard Appignanesi

Printed and bound in Australia
by McPherson's Printing Group, Victoria

Is Fascism Over?

Many people believe that Fascism ceased to be of any real political importance after 1945. Towards the end of the 20th century, however, Fascist parties were emerging, active and growing. Can we be sure that in the 21st century, Fascism will really be a thing of the past?

"Fascist" has become an all-purpose word. We often use it to describe people and things we dislike. It is applied indiscriminately to figures in authority, to modes of behaviour, to ways of thinking, to kinds of architecture.

What "Fascists" have in common is that they are the enemies of liberal or left-wing thought and attitudes. They can be seen as threatening, aggressive, repressive, narrowly conservative and blindly patriotic.

But this catch-all use of the word raises obvious questions. Are all people who could be defined in these terms really "Fascists"? Are all right-wing parties or groups, all conservative right-wing governments, necessarily "Fascist"?

What is Fascism?

Italy was the first country to have a party that called itself Fascist. The Italian word **fascio** (pronounced "fasho") means a bundle -of firewood, for instance. It was first used in the 1890s by workers in the notorious Sicilian sulphur mines.

FASCIO - SOMETHING DIFFICULT TO BREAK IF IT KEEPS TOGETHER

A UNION IN OTHER WORDS.

WE HIJACKED THE WORD FROM THE LEFT - LIKE SO MUCH ELSE!

In Italy after World War I the name was taken over by right-wing nationalistic groups who formed **fasci di combattimento** (combat squads). They came together in 1922 to found the first Fascist Party.

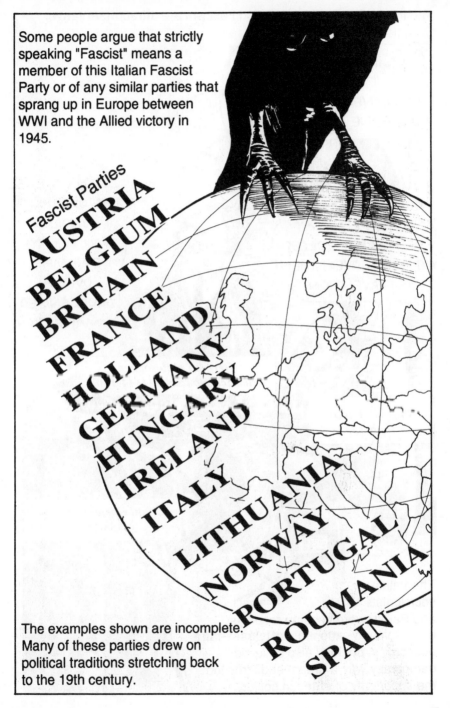

Some people argue that strictly speaking "Fascist" means a member of this Italian Fascist Party or of any similar parties that sprang up in Europe between WWI and the Allied victory in 1945.

Fascist Parties
AUSTRIA
BELGIUM
BRITAIN
FRANCE
HOLLAND
GERMANY
HUNGARY
IRELAND
ITALY
LITHUANIA
NORWAY
PORTUGAL
ROUMANIA
SPAIN

The examples shown are incomplete. Many of these parties drew on political traditions stretching back to the 19th century.

Ultraconservatism

The intellectual traditions behind Fascism are **ultraconservative.**

OUR IDEAL IS TO ACHIEVE THE SUPERMAN BY COLLECTIVE EXPERIMENTS IN DISCIPLINE AND BREEDING.

OUR BOTTOM-LINE IS THE FREE PLAY OF MARKET FORCES WITHOUT GOVERNMENT INTERVENTION.

THE ORGANIZED MINORITY WILL ALWAYS TRIUMPH OVER A DISORGANIZED MAJORITY.

German philosopher Friedrich Nietzsche (1844-1900)

Vilfredo Pareto (1848-1923)

Count Gaetano Mosca (1858-1941)

The Italian sociologists Mosca and Pareto were in some respects old-fashioned exponents of **laissez-faire** economics, but they also believed democracy was a dream and stressed the superiority of **elites** in society.

Besides being anti-democratic, ultraconservative thinkers were virulently opposed to socialism which was steadily developing in the 1880s. Socialism had its roots in the 18th century intellectual movement of the Enlightenment and the French Revolution.

WE REJECT SOCIALISM'S ANALYSIS OF THE CLASS NATURE OF SOCIETY!

Socialism's remedies to injustices and oppression, its opposition to war and its internationalism, were condemned as materialist, unpatriotic and weak.

The Ultraconservatives and Racism

Ultraconservatives embraced the notions of ideologues like the Frenchman, Count Joseph Gobineau (1816-82), in his **Essay on the Inequality of the Human Race** (1853).

RACES WHICH RETAIN THEIR PURITY ARE SUPERIOR TO OTHERS. BEST OF ALL IS THE ARYAN RACE.

I FIRST COINED THE TERM ANTI-SEMITISM AND SPOKE OF RACIAL CONFLICT. JEWISH ASSIMILATION MUST BE REJECTED AS DANGEROUS!

Houston Stewart Chamberlain (1885-1927), Wagner's son-in-law, an Englishman but naturalized German, was a leading theorist of German racial superiority and Jewish inferiority.

In 1873, Wilhelm Marr published **The Victory of Judaism over Germanism.**

OF COURSE, WE GERMANS BELONG TO THE PURE ARYAN RACE!

11

Ultraconservatives in France were fiercely patriotic, anti-republican and nostalgic for past glories. An example was Charles Maurras (1868-1952), the Catholic, monarchist and anti-Semite who hated Freemasons, Protestants and foreigners resident in France.

DEMOCRACY IS ANARCHY! IT IS FEMININE, WEAK, EVIL

I AGREE. THIS REPUBLIC IS DOMINATED BY JEWS. BUT WE MUST DO MORE THAN WRITE ABOUT IT. WE MUST GET TO THE PEOPLE IN THE STREETS!

Nietzsche

Edouard Drumont (1844-1917) writer of a notorious racist book, **La France Juive (Jewish France)**, published in 1886.
He also edited a popular anti-Semitic daily, **La Libre Parole.**

Wagner and other intellectuals in Germany had made anti-Semitic nationalism fashionable and respectable, at least on one level of "high culture". But how could ultraconservatism occupy the popular level and capture the imagination of the nation as a whole?

Ultraconservatives like Maurras and Drumont were also looking for an excuse to transfer anti-Semitism from the academic level to the streets and strengthen the "traditional Christian order" of France.

Nostalgic monarchists, Catholics and the army with its reactionary caste-system were allied against the liberals of the Third Republic, third generation offspring of the 1789 French Revolution.

The ultraconservative allies sought to challenge and undermine the legacy of the Enlightenment and republicanism which enshrined the radical ideals of Liberty, Equality and Fraternity, and thereby re-establish traditional authority.

The opportunity arose in France in 1894

The Dreyfus Affair

In 1894, Captain Alfred Dreyfus, sole Jewish member of the French general staff, was accused of spying for Germany.

WE SENTENCE YOU TO LIFE IMPRISONMENT ON DEVIL'S ISLAND.

THE EVIDENCE USED AGAINST ME IS A FORGERY!

INNOCENT

GUILTY

For 12 years, France was the scene of violent conflict between pro- and anti-Dreyfusards which became the focus of worldwide attention.

EVEN AFTER I WAS PARDONED AT MY RE-TRIAL IN 1899, THE STRUGGLE WENT ON - UNTIL MY NAME WAS FINALLY CLEARED IN 1906.

In 1897, the novelist Emile Zola (1840-1902) wrote his internationally famous **J'Accuse** (I Accuse) for a reopening of the case.

I WAS TRIED FOR LIBEL, CONVICTED AND FLED TO ENGLAND.

I WAS ELECTED TO THE CHAMBER OF DEPUTIES IN 1898 AND CAMPAIGNED AGAINST DREYFUS.

To the ultraconservatives, Dreyfus the Jew represented everything liberal and alien that conspired to "de-Christianize" society.

Edouard Drumont

I BECAME AN ARCHETYPE, A SCAPEGOAT - NO LONGER A HUMAN BEING!

The Dreyfus case split public opinion - in France but elsewhere too - along lines that determined political attitudes right up to the period of French collaboration with Hitler in World War II. It ranged liberals and socialists against the Racialist right and in defence of the Republic.
Although the case ended with the defeat of an organized, official French anti-Semitism, it left deep wounds, enduring bitterness and a hate for Jews.
It was a dress rehearsal for Hitlerism.

Another Forgery

Forgery was used to convict **one** Jewish individual of "conspiracy"–Dreyfus. Another far more dangerous forgery emerged in 1903 to convict **all** Jews of a "worldwide conspiracy". This was **The Protocols of the Elders of Zion** concocted by Russian agents in the Tsarist secret police working in Paris during the Dreyfus Affair.

WE FORGED THE EVIDENCE OF A JEWISH WORLD CONSPIRACY PLANNED AT SECRET MEETINGS OF THE FIRST ZIONIST CONGRESS IN 1897.

Despite repeated exposures of the fraud, **The Protocols** passed as genuine and were often republished.

I PUBLICIZED THE PROTOCOLS IN MY NEWSPAPER, THE DEARBORN INDEPENDENT.

Henry Ford
(1863-1947)
car manufacturer
and admirer of Hitler.

...and Pogroms

This campaign of anti-Semitic propaganda went in step with widespread **pogroms** during the late 19th and early 20th centuries in the region with the largest Jewish population in the Tsarist empire. It was known as the Pale of Settlement where Jews were massed together in Russia.

In 1905, the **Union of the Russian People,** a right-wing organization, began to speak of the need for the physical extermination of the Jews.

The Stage Is Set for World War One

Anti-Semitism, xenophobia and fervent nationalism were in place before the First World War was declared on 1 August 1914.

A strange, feverish mass hysteria
gripped the "civilized world"
at the outbreak of the war.

By 1914, Europe already had a climate of opinion that would favour
the rise of post-war Fascism.

The Breeding-Ground of Fascism

Post-war economic conditions were desperately bad in Germany, Italy and elsewhere. Unemployment and inflation struck hard at the middle class professionals and pensioners on fixed incomes. Large numbers of ex-soldiers felt they had been let down by civilian politicians.

In society in general there were discontented masses - unemployed, unwanted and excluded from the parliamentary game. They were ready to be recruited by parties offering an alternative - by violence if necessary - to corrupt democracy.

DISGUSTING! VIOLENCE IS THE ONLY WAY WE'LL ACHIEVE ANYTHING NOW!

Fascism as a mass political phenomenon was the response of the European upper and middle classes to a series of threats: recession, mass unrest, the Russian revolution, the organized working class and its left-wing parties.

The Italian Model

Italy in the early 1920s was in economic and political crisis. Hopes were frustrated that the sacrifices of the war would be rewarded by social reforms. Industrial workers and peasants arose in widespread strikes and demonstrations against living conditions.

Italian ex-servicemen and officers from the middle class were angry that although the country had fought on the winning side, it had not gained its just reward in the form of territories in the Mediterranean and colonies in Africa.

THE POST-WAR SETTLEMENT IS A MUTILATED VICTORY!

NOW WE'RE FACING UNEMPLOYMENT AND IMPOVERISHMENT!

WHAT HAVE WE AND OUR DEAD COMRADES SACRIFICED OURSELVES FOR?

WE'LL NEVER FORGIVE THE SOCIALISTS FOR OPPOSING ITALY'S ENTRY INTO THE WAR!

Most importantly, the Liberal government of the day and the forces of the Left were in deadlock.

In this atmosphere Benito Mussolini (1893-1945), an ex-socialist, journalist and ex-frontline soldier, emerged as a founder of the squads of ex-combatants and their supporters in blackshirt uniforms.

In 1922, the Fascists numbered almost a quarter of a million.
After a largely symbolic "March on Rome", Mussolini, who arrived by train, became head of government at the invitation of King Victor Emmanuel III.

IF WE CAN GET AWAY WITH KILLING MATTEOTTI, WE CAN GET AWAY WITH ANYTHING!

By 1926, parliamentary government had been abolished.

Giacomo Matteotti
1885-1924
The leading Socialist member of Parliament

There was strict censorship. The secret police OVRA was given wide powers. Special courts dealt with political prisoners. Some were executed. Many more received long sentences or were sent into internal exile in remote places.

The brilliant Marxist thinker Antonio Gramsci (1891-1937) spent long years in prison and died there.

FOR 20 YEARS WE MUST STOP THIS BRAIN FROM FUNCTIONING!

State Public Prosecutor

A Totalitarian or Corporative State

ITALY IS A TOTALITARIAN STATE IN WHICH THE POWER AND IDEOLOGY OF FASCISM CANNOT BE CHALLENGED.

SCRIPT BY GIOVANNI GENTILE

DIRECTOR

The totalitarian state envisaged by Italian Fascists, theorists like the philosopher Giovanni Gentile (1875-1944), was a **corporative state.** Employers and labour united and regulated in the interests of society as a whole. Workers and employers organized vertically in the same organizations with a common interest in productivity. Total control of the economy and the state by the Party.

IN FACT, THE ATTEMPT AT "TOTAL CONTROL" WAS RESISTED BY US - THE BIG BUSINESS INTERESTS!

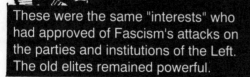

These were the same "interests" who had approved of Fascism's attacks on the parties and institutions of the Left. The old elites remained powerful.

Nostalgia and Imperialism

The Fascist Party adopted as its badge the **fasces** - the Latin word from which **fascio** is derived.

FASCES

A bundle of rods (for whipping people) round an axe (for capital punishment) carried in front of the rulers of Ancient Rome.

Adopting the fasces meant that Italy claimed the role of the Roman Empire.

IT MEANS CHALLENGING BRITISH DOMINATION OF THE MEDITERRANEAN! THE MEDITERRANEAN IS OUR SEA - THE MARE NOSTRUM OF THE ROMANS.

Fascist Italy was described in Fascist propaganda as a "proletarian nation" which had been denied its share of colonial wealth and territory to which it could export its unemployed and impoverished peasantry.

To this end, Fascist Italy adopted an economic policy of self-sufficiency - **autarchy** - and the regulation of large sections of industry with state intervention and funding.

Italy's leading industrialists, like those running the car manufacturing firm FIAT, were willing to put up with Fascism.

HEAVY INDUSTRY CAN ONLY PROSPER WITH THE REARMAMENT PROGRAMME.

AND BY BUILDING A STRONG FLEET.

WE'RE REDUCING UNEMPLOYMENT!

War came in the 1930s in Abyssinia, in Spain (in the Civil War on the side of Spanish Fascism) and in 1940 on the side of Germany in World War II.

29

The Fascist Party soon abandoned those elements in its programme which were critical of capitalism or supported reforms of conditions for workers.

The Italian Fascist Party was not initially anti-Semitic. Indeed, some Jews in the army, finance and industry were at first enthusiastic Fascists. But in 1936, Germany formed the so-called **Rome-Berlin Axis** by treaty, one which Japan joined later.

IT FAILED TO GAIN WIDE ACCEPTANCE AMONG THE ITALIAN PEOPLE.

ANTI-SEMITISM IS NOW OFFICIAL POLICY!

Italian Fascism embraced the theory of leadership by an elite. Power comes from the top down.
Believe, Obey, Fight!

The Head of State and of the Party is the Leader - **Il Duce** (pronounced Doo-chay).

CREDERE
OBBEDIRE
COMBATTERE

Italian Fascism collapsed with the defeat of the German forces in Italy in 1945 and the execution of Mussolini by Resistance fighters.

From this collapse the old power elites in industry, finance, the Church and in many areas of law enforcement and the military, emerged intact. The social and economic system of Italy was unchanged.

The German Model

As in Italy, national pride in Germany had been wounded by the peace terms imposed by the WWI Allies - headed by France, the USA and Britain. This was the hated **Diktat** - the dictated peace settlement of Versailles, 1919.

AND US, THE *FREIKORPS!*

The **Freikorps** (Free Corps) were ruthless right-wing military formations operating independently.

BECAUSE THEY OPPOSED THE WAR AND WANT A SOVIET GERMANY!

BECAUSE THEY BETRAYED GERMANY BY SIGNING THE PEACE TREATIES!

The Freikorps murdered their political opponents - notably the Communists **Karl Leibknecht** (1871-1919) **and Rosa Luxemburg** (1887-1919).

Bourgeois politicians of the Centre, like the Foreign Minister **Walter Rathenau** (1887-1922), were also assassinated.

By supporting the government, the army won a position of great power and independence in the German state.

In this atmosphere of inflation, unemployment and insecurity, the **National Socialist German Workers' Party** - the Nazi Party - emerged. It promised many things.

Supporting **the little man** the peasant, artisan, small businessman.

Attacking the **bondage of interest** imposed by the banks and big business (meaning Jewish firms).

Putting the **weal of the community** before the weal of the individual.

Opposing the **socialism of the Left** by a **national socialism of the Right.**

Creating **social unity** in the cause of the German people - **das Volk.**

Das Volk was a concept based on myths of the German race, a Teutonic legendary past, Wagner's operas and figures like Hermann, the chief who fought the Roman legions.

Adolf Hitler (1889-1945) the Nazi Party organizer was, like Mussolini, an ex-combatant and frontline soldier. His involvement in a 1923 right-wing **putsch** ended in total failure. Hitler was imprisoned for a short time.

Hitler's party did not become crucially important until the world economic crisis of the 1930s.

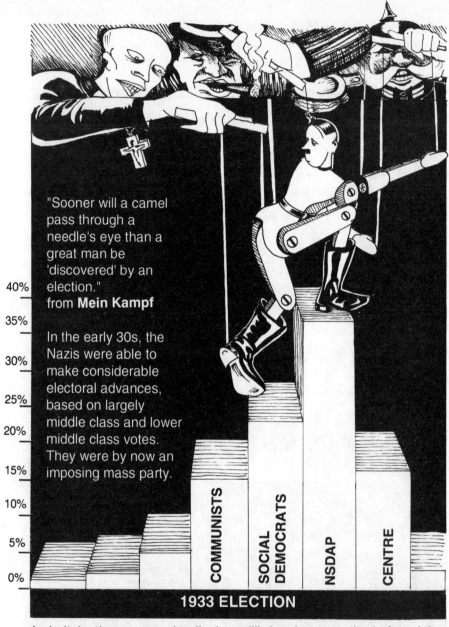

"Sooner will a camel pass through a needle's eye than a great man be 'discovered' by an election."
from **Mein Kampf**

In the early 30s, the Nazis were able to make considerable electoral advances, based on largely middle class and lower middle class votes. They were by now an imposing mass party.

40%
35%
30%
25%
20%
15%
10%
5%
0%

COMMUNISTS

SOCIAL DEMOCRATS

NSDAP

CENTRE

1933 ELECTION

As in Italy, there was a deadlock equilibrium between the Left and the German government. By obtaining the support of an important number of industrialists, right-wing politicians and the army, Hitler was able to present himself as a suitable candidate for the Chancellorship and head of government.

Hitler was **legally** installed as Chancellor in 1933 with the support of conservatives who hoped the Nazis would crush the Left. They believed themselves able to control the Nazis.

The Left was divided and confused. In the last free election in 1933 the Nazis still did not win an overall majority - they received only 43% of the total vote - but they had been **given** the power.

The Instrument is Terror

The Nazis' first steps included the abolition of trade unions and left-wing parties.

Concentration camps were set up and immediately filled with their political opponents - Communists,Socialists,critics of Nazism.

SIEG
SIEG HEIL
SIEG HEIL
SIEG HEIL
SIEG HEIL
SIEG HEIL
SIEG HIEL
SIEG HEIL

Education, the Church, culture, were brought under Nazi control. The Party was all-powerful. Germany too, like Italy, was a totalitarian state with a formalized leadership - Hitler as supreme leader - the Fuehrer

I AM GERMANY AND GERMANY IS ME...
..HOW FORTUNATE THAT WE HAVE FOUND EACH OTHER !

Purging the Brownshirt Storm Troopers

A tendency in the Nazi Party wished to insist on the radical "socialist" anti-capitalist element. This was the party's militia, the brown-shirted SA (**Sturmabteilung** or Storm Troopers). The SA commander Ernst Roehm (1881-1934) was a homosexual.

THAT'S A GOOD MORAL EXCUSE!

Roehm and other SA leaders were shot in a purge called "the Night of the Long Knives" in 1934.

Power now passed to the elite corps of the SS (**Schutzstaffel**) originally created by Hitler as his Black Shirt personal bodyguard, but in 1929 put under the command of Heinrich Himmler who made the SS the most feared organization in Europe.

What remained of "socialism" after the SA purge was a policy of mobilization for social ends in organizations like the Labour Front, used on public works like the autobahns, or the Hilter Youth Movement.

Welfare programmes for workers were organized by the Strength through Joy Movement.

holidays, cruises, sports events, model housing for workers

a cheap "people's radio" a cheap "people's car" - the Volkswagen

The Survival of the Fittest

NOT SOCIALISM - BUT SOCIAL DARWINISM!

Racism was central to Nazi thinking and policies based on the theory of **eugenics** - a misleading and dangerous idea of Darwinian "natural selection" applied to society.

Eugenics was invented in 1883 by Francis Galton (1822-1911) a British scientist.

BREEDING BETWEEN PEOPLE OF HIGH INTELLIGENCE WILL IMPROVE THE QUALITY OF THE RACE.

OUR LIFE'S WORK FOR EUGENIC BREEDING AND THE RACE.

Dr Marie Stopes (1880-1958) birth-control pioneer.

I PROPOSE THAT 100,000 MORALLY DEGENERATE BRITONS SHOULD BE FORCIBLY STERILIZED AND OTHERS PUT IN LABOUR CAMPS TO HALT THE DECLINE OF THE BRITISH RACE.

Winston Churchill (1874-1965) as Home Secretary in a 1910 Departmental Paper.

The author and playwright George Bernard Shaw (1856-1950) was another of the many supporters of this racist doctrine.

45

The Logic of the Holocaust

In 1926, the American Eugenics Society advocated the sterilization of the insane, the retarded and epileptics.

The Nazis began by applying the principles of eugenics to the mentally disabled, who were the first victims to be "experimentally gassed" -some 200,000 adults and children between 1939 and 1941.

Homosexuals were also classed as unacceptably deviant, while gypsies and Slavs were classified as racially inferior.

Homosexuals, gypsies and Slavs died in large numbers in labour and extermination camps during World War 2.

"Ethnic Cleansing"

This same bogus genetic theory maintained that the Jews were a threat to the "pure Aryan stock" of the Germans.

"Jews are an alien body that creates ill-feeling, disease, ever- festering sores - death. These aliens are the cause of putrefaction and should be destroyed as quickly and thoroughly as possible."
Orientalist and Biblical scholar Paul de Lagarde (1827-1891).

Germany had to be made **Judenrein** - purged of Jews.
Apart from the "genetic threat", Jews were labelled as doubly dangerous - both as powerful capitalists and subversive Bolsheviks. To get rid of Jews would remove threats from two directions at once. This absurd proposition in due course found its logical result in the Holocaust.

A War Economy

The Nazi leadership embarked on a policy of territorial expansion leading to war

AND WE "ARYAN" BUSINESSMEN GOT CONFISCATED JEWISH PROPERTIES AT KNOCKDOWN PRICES!

SOLVES THE PROBLEM OF UNEMPLOYMENT!

HEAVY INDUSTRY PROSPERS UNDER STATE INTERVENTION AND DIRECTION.

German industry was from the first complicit in the Nazi regime.

When the extermination camps were set up in Poland in the 1940s, German firms like **Siemens** and **IG Farben** built factories alongside them.

BMW, the Bavarian car-manufacturing company, used slave labour from Dachau. **Degesch**, a pesticide manufacturer, supplied Zyklon B for the gas chambers. The firm of **Topf & Son** designed the cremation ovens (and took out a patent on its system in 1953!)

The camps were a source of cheap expendable labour. So too were conquered territories of the East from which slave-labour was imported to work in industry and on the land.

The End of Hitler's "Thousand-Year" Reich

Nazism collapsed with the total defeat of the German military machine. Germany was divided - a political reality of which the Berlin Wall became the symbol.

In West Germany
The British, French and American allies restored a capitalist economy which had suffered physical destruction but was still quickly rebuilt.

The old pre-Nazi elites were still intact and ready to resume their place in the Federal Republic.

In East Germany
The Russians installed their Stalinist version of a "socialist" command economy and a totalitarian state system.

But what was under this "socialist" veneer, waiting to come out?

The Spanish Model

Spain was the third European country to have a Fascist government. It came to power as the result of a military rebellion and a civil war which lasted from 1936 to 1939.

1931 saw the free election of a Republican government committed to social reform.

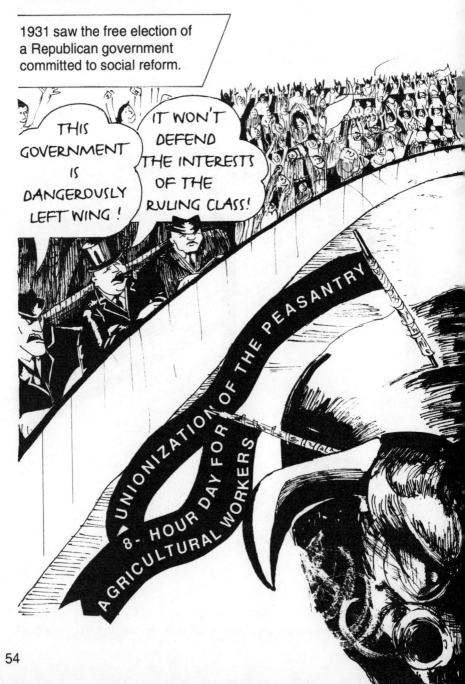

THIS GOVERNMENT IS DANGEROUSLY LEFT WING!

IT WON'T DEFEND THE INTERESTS OF THE RULING CLASS!

UNIONIZATION OF THE PEASANTRY

8-HOUR DAY FOR AGRICULTURAL WORKERS

The most prominent of these parties was the Falange (literally, the Phalanx) founded in 1933 by Primo de Rivera (1903-36) and modelled on the Italian Fascist Party. Rivera was assassinated.

Falangist Style

blue shirt, Fascist rituals, Fascist salute, Fascist chants

Spanish Fascism was nostalgic.

The Catholic majesties, Ferdinand and Isabella, reigned 1479-1504.

AH, THE GOLDEN AGE OF THE SPANISH EMPIRE!

WE DROVE THE MOORS FROM SPAIN, EXPELLED THE JEWS AND FINANCED COLUMBUS WHO OPENED UP THE AMERICAS TO COLONIALISM.

The Falangist badge featured the emblem of the Catholic Kings - a bundle of arrows (a version of the **fascio**) - and the black and red colours borrowed from the radical left-wing anarcho-syndicalism.

In the ideological field, Fascism maintained that Spain had been corrupted by the ideas of the Enlightenment and the French Revolution.

El Moviemento

The election in 1936 of a Popular Front Government made up of Socialists, Communists and Radicals, triggered a military rebellion led by General Francisco Franco (1892-1975).

WE'LL BEGIN HERE IN SPANISH MOROCCO WHERE THE ARMY HAS A STRONG BASE AFTER FIGHTING A LONG COLONIAL WAR

Franco forced the Fascists and Monarchists into a single organization, together with the army, to form the **Moviemento.**

OF WHICH FRANCO IS OUR <u>CAUDILLO</u> (THE LEADER).

AND HE'S THE <u>JEFE</u> (THE CHIEF) OF OUR FALANGE.

The Civil War ended after 3 years with Franco's victory.

A victory made possible by the expeditionary units of the German and Italian army, navy and airforce.

Irish Fascists, French Monarchists and White Russian exiles also fought for the rebels, but were far fewer in number than the International Brigades.

IT WAS BAD NEWS FOR DEMOCRACY WHEN NO OTHER COUNTRY EXCEPT RUSSIA HELPED THE SPANISH REPUBLIC!

I WITNESSED AND WROTE ABOUT THE MURDER OF LEFTISTS IN BARCELONA—

BUT WASN'T BELIEVED!

Stalin's help included sending Comintern agents to purge his enemies – Trotskyists, anarchists and radicals – thereby causing a "civil war within a civil war" on the Left and weakening the Republican effort.

George Orwell (1903-50) in **Homage to Catalonia.**

The victory of Fascism in the Civil War was followed by a dictatorial regime with concentration camps, forced labour for opponents of the regime, and special courts which handed out summary death sentences in appalling numbers.

With the destruction of the Left, the peasants and workers were left defenceless in the face of attacks on wages and living standards. The trade unions were handed over to the Falange which also inherited the printing presses and other property of the Left.

40 Years of Fascist Dictatorship

When military victory had been won, Franco distanced himself from the Falange, whose prestige was undermined by the collapse of Italian Fascism in 1943 to which the Falange was linked.

YOU SHOULDN'T BACK LOSERS!

BUT WE'RE STILL A FORCE IN INTERNAL POLITICS....

POWER REMAINS WITH US!

The Falange controlled a mass Youth Movement. It also penetrated the civil service and dispensed patronage in many areas of Spanish life.

The military

Rightwing Catholics and technocrats from the Opus Dei - a powerful, secretive Catholic organization which still has important connections in politics, industry and finance in and outside Spain.

The Fascist dictatorship was gradually eroded by Spain's growing economic prosperity, and by the pressure of the US which wanted air-bases in Spain.

LET'S CALL IT PERMANENT MILITARY TOURISM.

AND WE CAN SEE THAT THE REGIME'S TRADITIONALIST VIEWS AND CONTROL OF THE ECONOMY ARE HINDERING THE COUNTRY'S DEVELOPMENT.

Financiers and industrialists.

On Franco's death in 1975, the monarchy was restored. Once again the old elites were still in place.

Other Brands of European Fascism

Fascism in the interwar years had many national varieties. It was chameleon-like, drawing on different local right-wing and radical traditions.

In France, there were anti-Semitic organizations like the Monarchist **Action Française** and Fascist leagues like the **Croix de Feu** composed of veterans decorated for bravery in World War 1.

In Belgium, the Fascists were **Rexists** - followers of **Christus Rex** (Christ the King), Catholic and nationalist. **In Roumania**, the **Iron Guard** was fanatically religious and nationalistic.

In Hungary, the **Arrow Cross** was Christian, nationalist and anti-Semitic.

Then there were varieties of Fascism best defined as clerical Fascism. Examples were the long, puritanically religious dictatorship of Antonio Oliveira Salazar (1889-1970) in **Portugal** and **Austria** in the 30s, before Hitler took over, experienced the brief regime of Chancellor Engelbert Dolfuss, a Catholic, anti-socialist and anti-Semite.

The British Case

The insecurity and mass unemployment caused by the Great Depression of the 1930s help to explain the rise of Fascism in some European countries. Britain shared the same problems, but Fascism had only a very moderate success.

Oswald Mosley (1896-1980) who emerged as the leader of a Fascist party had been a soldier in the 1914-18 war.

I STARTED MY POLITICAL LIFE AS A TORY BUT PASSED OVER TO THE LABOUR PARTY AND HELD A MINOR CABINET POST.

BUT THE LABOUR GOVERNMENT REFUSED TO ADOPT RADICAL MEASURES TO END UNEMPLOYMENT...

So, Mosley founded the New Party. Not a success. So he went on to found the **British Union of Fascists**, drawing on a tradition of nationalist racism that stemmed from the 1904 British Brothers League, created to reduce or stop immigration from Eastern Europe.

Mosley was also typical in being funded by a big industrialist, Sir William Morris, the car manufacturer, and encouraged by Lord Rothermere, owner of the **Daily Mail** which supported the Blackshirts.

WE'LL ESTABLISH A CORPORATIVE STATE AND CUT THROUGH THE MUDDLES OF DEMOCRACY!

OUR PARTY BADGE IS THE _FASCES_ BECAUSE THE ROMAN EMPIRE TODAY IS BRITISH!

The BUF was never more than 40-thousand strong at its peak in the 30s. Its members came overwhelmingly from the lower middle-class - small shopkeepers, students, unemployed. But it did have a measure of working-class support - up to 20% of the vote in local elections in parts of East London which had a large Jewish community.

Reasons for the Failure of Fascism
in Pre-war Britain

One reason for the BUF's small impact on British political life was that Mosley's brand of jingoistic anti-Semitism could comfortably find a home in the right wing of the Conservative Party.

What did the politically important sections of the Right think in the 1930s?

Britain was also fortunate that the bulk of its armed forces were stationed abroad in the Empire and thus removed from the political arena. We should remember what happened at the Curragh in 1914 - the officer corps mutinied in protest against granting Home Rule to Ireland!

Mosley's blackshirt Fascists held mass rallies at which interrupters were severely manhandled, with the police apparently unwilling to intervene.

In 1936, the Public Order Act forbade the wearing of uniforms and gave the police greater powers to control public demonstrations and marches - powers used as much against the Left as against Fascism.

The Battle of Cable Street

If on the Conservative Right the BUF was seen as too extreme and politically unnecessary, on the Left there was a willingness to challenge the Blackshirts openly. Of this, the prime example is the battle of Cable Street in 1937.

Mosley's Fascists planned a march through a Jewish area of the East End. The Labour Party kept aloof and advised its members not to resist the march. The police intervened against the demonstrators who forced the Fascists to turn back. It was a crucial victory for the Left.

In 1940, the BUF was declared illegal and Mosley was interned along with the leaders of other smaller Fascist groups.

The Axis Domination of Europe

When most of Europe fell under the domination of the Rome-Berlin Axis, local Fascist parties and governments were encouraged.

In the unoccupied zone of France a collaborationist government was set up in the town of Vichy, headed by Field-Marshal Philippe Pétain (1856-1951), a legendary military figure from the 1914-18 war.

WE REPLACED THE REPUBLICAN MOTTO "LIBERTY, EQUALITY, FRATERNITY" BY "FATHERLAND, WORK, FAMILY".

Celtic axes took the place of Marianne, symbol of the Republic. And the French Republic became the "French State".

The Vichy militia and police were zealous in hunting down Jews and members of the Resistance.
Pétain's regime strove to present an image of a certain independence from Nazi Germany, but it was a loyal Fascist collaborator.

WE DIDN'T HAVE TO FORCE THEM TO PASS ANTI-SEMITIC LAWS.

There were also puppet or quisling governments in Norway, Holland, Belgium and Slovakia. The anti-Semitic priest, Father **Josef Tiso** (1887-1947), headed the Slovak Fascist government. In Croatia, the Ustashis under **Ante Palevic** set up a Fascist regime. All of them collapsed with the defeat of the Nazi armies. Many of their members - Tiso was one - were executed as war criminals and collaborators. Many were imprisoned. But many others survived to keep alive the political faith in Fascism.

The Case of Japan

The Imperial regime that led Japan into World War 2 has been variously described as "Fascist", "militarist", "ultra-nationalist", "totalitarian".

Japan in the 30s was one of the oddest places on earth. It was headed by a divinity, the Emperor. It was a semi-feudal capitalist state with a politically important hereditary nobility.

The economic sector was dominated by the **zaibatsu** (financial cliques) made up of large cartels, such as Mitsubishi, Nissan and others in finance and industry, which acted in part as agents of government.

The government itself consisted of shifting coalitions between the **zaibatsu,** the elite bureaucracy which ran the country for the Emperor, and the armed forces drawn mainly from the land - the soldiers from the peasantry, the officers from the small landowners. The hereditary nobility in the House of Peers played a key role as mediators between these groups and the Imperial Court.

Japan was a colonial power. It had conquered Korea, gained Taiwan and received some German possessions in the Pacific as a reward for fighting on the Allied side in World War 1.

Japan's policy of expansion was supported by the zaibatsu, the high command of the armed forces, and in secret the Emperor himself.

Recession and Rebellion

In 1931 a group of rebellious army officers precipitated an invasion of Manchuria in north west China.

In 1932, some radical agrarian conspirators murdered Prime Minister Inukai and the tycoon, Baron Dan.

THIS WAY WE ASSERT OUR POWER AGAINST THE ECONOMIC CRISIS WHICH IS DESTROYING FARMERS AND SMALL BUSINESSMEN.

THIS WAY WE FREE THE EMPEROR FROM EVIL ADVISORS RESPONSIBLE FOR AGRARIAN SUFFERING AND NATIONAL WEAKNESS.

The Niniroku

The **niniroku** or Incident of 26 February 1936 was a major army uprising in Tokyo led by a militant faction which aimed to liquidate the ruling elite and reform the nation.

The **niniroku** conspirators were influenced by **Kita Ikki** (1884–1937), a right-wing revolutionary and founder of Japanese Fascism, who was executed for his part in the plot.

I WAS INSPIRED BY CHINA'S NATIONAL RENEWAL. MY TACTICS BORROW FROM LENIN AND HITLER-- A BLEND OF BOLSHEVISM AND NATIONAL SOCIALISM ADAPTED TO JAPANESE TRADITIONS OF EMPEROR WORSHIP.

Kita Ikki was a professional agitator who had served with Sun Yat-sen's nationalist revolutionaries in China during the 1911 toppling of the Manchu dynasty.

Kita Ikki's **Plan for the Reorganization of Japan** had been printed and circulated secretly for many years, although banned by the police. It envisaged a radically transformed Japan leading a revolutionary movement that would sweep through Asia, challenging modern capitalism, confronting the Western colonial powers, in particular the USA.

Kita Ikki's **Reorganization** aimed at "national renovation" based on the ideal of a "people's Emperor", a divine symbol of community and freedom from corrupt bureaucrats. Here are some of his planned reforms:

- Abolition of the peerage and universal manhood suffrage (literally "manhood", since women would be excluded from politics).

- Redistribution of surplus land to the peasantry.

- Confiscation of industrial capital transferred to the state to curtail the power of the **zaibatsu.**

- Nationalization of major industries.

- Industrial production and management run by state agencies.

- An 8-hour working day and a limit on incomes.

Kita Ikki envisaged a corporate state on the Italian model.

The **niniroku** was destined to fail. The Emperor's inner circle of military and political top brass took advantage of the failed coup to purge the army of dissidents and prepare it for conquest.

THE REALLY SUCCESSFUL CONSPIRATORS OF THE 1930S WERE THOSE IN COMMAND OF THE COUNTRY, WHIPPING UP NATIONALIST FEELINGS IN PRELUDE TO WAR!

Before Pearl Harbour

What were the typically Fascist strategies of Japan's Imperial regime?

- Attack the left-wing parties and unions.

- Reduce the Diet (Japanese parliament) to impotence.

- Introduce severe censorship enforced by the **kempeitai** - the Gestapo-style "thought police".

- Appeal to ultranationalist Shinto mythology - the Sun Goddess and Emperor worship.

- Indoctrinate the Japanese people as a superior race.

- Militarize every aspect of society.

- Promote the armed forces to the function of mass party and "vanguard of the nation".

- Instil the militarist traditions and moral code of the **samurai,** the feudal knighthood - **bushido.**

- Demand total sacrifice from its elite warriors, such as the suicidal attacks by the Kamikaze on American warships.

- Elevate death as the true fulfilment of life.

- Keep women subservient.

The Greater East Asia Co-Prosperity Sphere

Kita Ikki's far-reaching programme of conquest was adopted by the Imperial regime and named **The Greater East Asia Co-Prosperity Sphere.** The following "Land Disposal Plan" issued by the Ministry of War in December 1941 will give some idea of the regime's ambitions.

I WAS SHOT FOR RIGHTWING EXTREMISM - BUT THE IMPERIAL REGIME WAS EQUALLY FASCIST IN ITS OWN PROGRAMME.

PLANS FOR THE NEW ORDER IN EAST ASIA AND THE SOUTH SEAS

1. Regions to be under the jurisdiction of the Government-General of Formosa:
Hong Kong
Macao (to be purchased)
The Philippine Islands
Paracel Islands
Hainan Island (to be purchased from China)

2. To be administered by the South Seas Government Office:
Guam
Nauru
Ocean Island
Gilbert Islands
Wake

3. The Melanesia Region Government-General or South Pacific Government-General (provisional titles):
New Guinea (the British and Australian mandated territories east of Long. 141 degrees E.)
The Admiralty Archipelago
New Britain, New Ireland and the islands in the vicinity
The Solomons
Santa Cruz Archipelago
Ellice Islands
Fiji Islands
New Hebrides
New Caledonia
Loyalty Island
Chesterfield Island

4. Eastern Pacific Government-General:
Hawaii
Howland, Baker and Phoenix Islands, Rain Islands Marquesas and Tuamotu Islands, Society Islands, Cook and Austral Islands
Samoa
Tonga
5. The Australian Government-General:
The whole of Australia and Tasmania
6. The New Zealand Government-General (provisional title):
The North and South Islands of New Zealand
Macquarie Island
The sea, south of the Tropic of Capricorn and east of Long. 160 degrees E., as far as the S. Pole region
7. The Ceylon Government-General:
Ceylon; and India lying south of the following boundary: from the west coast on the northern frontier of Portuguese Goa, thence to the north of Dharwar and Bellary and to the River Penner, and along the north bank of the Penner to the east coast at Nellore
Laccadive Islands
Maldive Islands
Chagos Islands
Seychelles
Mauritius
8. Alaska Government-General:
Alaska
The Yukon Province, and the land between that Province and the Mackenzie River
Alberta
British Columbia
The State of Washington
9. The Government-General of Central America:
Guatemala
San Salvador

Honduras
British Honduras
Nicaragua
Costa Rica
Panama
Colombia, and the Maracaibo district of Venezuela
Ecuador
Cuba
Haiti
Dominica
Jamaica
Bahamas
The future of Trinidad, British and Dutch Guiana and British and French possessions in the Leeward Islands to be decided by agreement between Japan and Germany after the war
10. In the event of her declaring war on Japan, Mexico to cede territory east of Long. 95 degrees 30'. Should Peru join the war against Japan it must cede territory north of Lat. 10 degrees; and if Chile enters the war it shall cede the nitre zone north of Lat. 24 degrees.

Independent States
1. The East Indies Kingdom:
All Dutch possessions in the E. Indies
British Borneo, Labuan, Sarawak, Brunei
Cocos
Christmas Island
Andamans
Nicobars
Portuguese Timor (to be purchased)
2. The Kingdom of Burma:
British Burma and Assam, together with part of Bengal between the Ganges and Brahmaputra
3. The Malay Kingdom
4. The Kingdom of Thailand
5. The Kingdom of Cambodia:
Cambodia and French Cochin China
6. The Kingdom of Annam:
Annam, Laos and Tongking

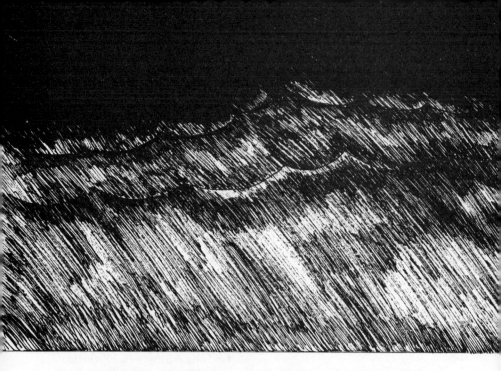

The militarist Imperial regime led the Japanese people to tragic disaster and total Unconditional Surrender.

A single napalm bombing of Tokyo on 10 March 1945 killed 124,000 people - higher than the A-bomb figures and over twice the total number of US battle dead for the entire war.

The Balance Sheet of Fascism

Facist regimes in Italy, Germany, Spain and Japan were superficially varied, drawing on different histories and traditions. But they had some or all of the following in common:

1. A political philosophy which was a compound of radical ideas and mysticism, of left-wing-sounding slogans and conservative policies.

2. A strong state with a powerful executive which did not require democratic consultation before acting, combined with a hatred of bourgeois democracy.

3. Hatred of Communism and Socialism as political movements based on the idea of class differences and class antagonisms. Against this idea, Fascism aimed to substitute a corporative state that denied a divergence of class interests between capital and labour.

4. The formation of a mass party on paramilitary lines which drew its recruits in part from the discontented and disenfranchised working-class

5. Admiration of power and the deed which found expression in the cult of violence. Training for war and violence gave free rein to sadistic and pathological characteristics.

6. Authoritarian programmes which emphasized conformity, discipline and submission. Society was militarized and directed by a messianic leader.

7. The cultivation of irrationality - the impulse was more important than logical thought. Irrationality led to a cult of death - witness the Spanish Fascist slogan: **Arriba la Muerte!** - Long live Death!

8. Nostalgia for the legendary past. For instance, in Italy's case, the Roman Empire. In Germany, an appeal to primitive myths of Nibelungen. The initials SS were written in Runic letters from Viking times. Japan resurrected the medieval code of the **samurai.**

9. Aversion to intellectuals whom Fascism accused of undermining the old certainties and traditional values.

10. Fascism claimed to honour the dignity of labour and the role of the peasantry as providers of the staples of life. With this went an idealized picture of rural life - the healthy countryside versus the decadent city.

11. Machismo. Women were relegated to traditional female roles as housewives, servants, nurses, and as breeders of "racially pure" warriors for the state war machine.

12. Fascism was frequently subsidized by big industrialists and landowners.

13. Fascism's electoral support came overwhelmingly from the middle-class - in particular the lower middle-class affected by economic crisis.

14. Fascism needed scapegoat enemies - "the Other" on whom to focus society's agressions and hates

The Essential Scapegoat of Fascism

In most societies across the world, "the Other" plays a crucially negative role. The Other can be a Protestant or Catholic, Hindu or Muslim, Serb or Croat, white or black, immigrant or AIDS victim. The Other is distinguished by racial and cultural differences which can include skin colour, beliefs, eating habits and sexual mores. The Other is by definition **different** and **inferior.**

Fascists cast various groups in this category of Otherness.

THE OTHER

BLACKS, GYPSIES, SLAVS, KOREANS and CHINESE on grounds of race.
HOMOSEXUALS on the grounds of deviance.
INTELLECTUALS because they have fancy ideas about culture.

WHEN I HEAR THE WORD *CULTURE* I REACH FOR MY REVOLVER!

Reich Marshal Hermann Goering.

For the European Fascist, the Jews embodied Otherness. Jews had their own religion, own culture, closed communities, dietary laws, rituals of dress and behaviour.

The Wannsee Conference

ON THE ONE HAND JEWS ARE FINANCIERS, OWNERS OF BIG STORES AND BUSINESS COMPETITORS....

ON THE OTHER, THEY SABOTAGE US BY LEFTWING ACTIVISM, JOURNALISM AND BY CONTROLLING THE ENTERTAINMENT INDUSTRY.

Jews were believed to be in league with each other all over the world, in control of international finance and international left-wing movements. In the paranoid view of the Nazis, this added up to a "Zionist conspiracy". Jews infected society and had to be swept away.

On 20 January 1942, Reinhard Heydrich, Chief of the Security Service (SD) and Hitler's favourite "hangman", called a conference of some 15 top-ranking Nazis at Wannsee near Berlin.

IN ACCORDANCE WITH THE FUEHRER'S STATED POLICIES, THE TIME HAS COME TO SOLVE THE JEWISH QUESTION _FINALLY._

THERE ARE SOME 11 MILLION JEWS INVOLVED IN THIS FINAL SOLUTION.

Even in Japan, where Jews were unknown, the regime invented a "Judeo-Masonic-Bolshevik" conspiracy to justify its attack on China. A Japanese delegate to the 1938 Weltdienst Congress in Germany declared....

JAPANESE SOLDIERS ARE DYING TO SAVE THE WHOLE WORLD FROM THIS CONSPIRACY!

What are the Attractions of Fascism?

Books, films and television have created many stereotypes of Fascism over the years. Fascists are portrayed as jack-booted, sadistic automatons. There is some truth in this caricature, but clearly it does not fit all the vast number of people who joined the Fascist parties. What attracted these "ordinary" people to Fascism?

FASCISM

Paradoxically, submersion in the mass gives you identity, the shared power of nationality and race. Fascism appeals to the romanticism of youth, the lure of self-sacrifice to a common cause, the rediscovery of comradeship in battle.

Social differences vanish in the unselfish experience of danger, discomfort and suffering.
Fascism gives you a clear and identifiable ENEMY!

The "Greenness" of Fascism

Fascism is marked by **nostalgia** - a longing for the "good times" before the industrial revolution. German culture especially has a tradition of 19th century Romanticism strongly critical of industrial society.

STRENGTH THROUGH JOY

Hitler Youth hiking through Germany in the 30s represented the "green" element in National Socialist ideology.

Male bonding was strong in the Hitler Youth and its Italian equivalent, the **Balilla.** There were also women's movements, like the Nazi **Bund deutscher Maedel** (League of Young German Women).

THE MEDIA - How Fascism Made Itself Attractive

Fascism came to power in an age when politicians still relied on mass meetings and oratory to inspire their followers.

But the press was already available as a political weapon, refined and exploited by both Left and Right.

WE MADE A FINE ART OF PUBLIC SPEAKING.

WE BOLSHEVIKS SMUGGLED OUR NEWSPAPER *ISKRA* INTO RUSSIA BEFORE THE 1917 REVOLUTION

AND AFTER, PAPERS LIKE *PRAVDA* AND *IZVESTIA* BECAME IMPORTANT PROPAGANDA INSTRUMENTS.

IN THE YEARS BEFORE 1914, I WAS EDITOR OF THE SOCIALIST PARTY'S NEWSPAPER *AVANTI!*

THE NAZI PARTY OWNS THE MASS CIRCULATION *VÖLKISCHER BEOBACHTER* - AND STRICTLY CONTROLS ALL THE PRESS!

The development of **agitprop** in revolutionary Russia exploited the new mass media of radio and film.
Radio could reach a wider audience than any public meeting - and it crossed frontiers!
But it was easily limited by government control.

Radio sets in wartime Italy were modified to pick up only official wavelengths... and then officially sealed!
The manufacture in Germany of the "people's radio" acknowledged its importance in communicating the Leader's speeches.

Film

In Italy, Germany and the Soviet Union, film as an instrument of propaganda was early recognized and exploited.

Under the Nazis, Germany's highly developed film industry produced mass entertainment films with propaganda themes (e.g. anti-Semitism, wholesome peasant life, heroic battles).

The documentary films of the highly skilled director Leni Riefensthal (1902-) aestheticized both the giant 1934 Nuremberg Nazi rally and the 1938 Berlin Olympic Games.

Compare the Nazi rally with Busby Berkeley's Hollywood musicals. Both exploit the choreography of **depersonalization.**

The Pornography of Death

German photographic equipment was highly advanced.
The first hand-held 16mm film cameras were used on all fronts.

German soldiers took endless "snaps" of shootings, hangings and gas chamber selections - the irrefutable evidence of genocide. This partly explains why the crimes of the German army and the SS are so fully documented. German POWs were often found with examples of this **pornography of death** as souvenirs.

Nazi visual recordings of suffering and death were the forerunners of today's porno "snuff movies" and the "reality television" now promoted by America's NBC network.

Signal, a wartime Nazi magazine of mass circulation in Occupied Europe, employed the latest developments in colour photography.

Signal presented its readers with propaganda images - "the Wehrmacht in its historic fight against Bolshevism" - "the heroism of German troops at the front".

Signal's layout techniques were adopted after the war by mass publications like **Paris Match**.

Fine Art

Although the Nazi economic programme favoured heavy industry over agriculture, themes of peasant life, honest labour and maternity were officially endorsed in the fine arts.

Another focus was the human figure, realistic and pompously heroic.

Male nudes were strongly coloured by homoeroticism. Female figures were anatomically precise, idealized versions of images in nudist magazines.

Eroticism that easily slips into pornography.

These "wholesome" images were supposed to combat the "degenerate art" of modernism.

YOU CAN'T GET A POSITIVE VIEW OF LIFE FROM THE DEGENERATE ART OF JEWS, BOLSHEVIKS AND NEGROES!

And what were the Nazis' "positive images" of life?

Nordic man and Nordic woman - blond, strong, athletic, heroic! The frontline soldier - severe, resolute, romantic!

A Nostalgia for the Future

Italy was less industrially advanced than Germany. Futurism, an early modernist movement, celebrated the machine age that would radically change backward Italy. Futurism, with its "nostalgia for the future", fed into Fascism. Its main theoretician was F.T. Marinetti who gloried the aesthetics of war and the beauty of aerial bombing.

From Marinetti's Futurist Manifesto (1909)

"We will glorify war - the world's only hygiene - militarism, patriotism, the destructive gesture of freedom bringers, beautiful ideas worth dying for, and scorn for woman."

"A racing car whose bonnet is adorned with great pipes like serpents of explosive breath - a roaring car that seems to ride on grapeshot - is more beautiful than the Victory of Samothrace."

"We shall sing a hymn to the man at the wheel, who hurls the lance of spirit across the earth along the circle of its orbit."

Caricature

Fascism exploited Europe's long and disgraceful tradition of anti-Semitic and racist caricature.

EVER SINCE SHAKESPEARE'S SHYLOCK.

Italian Fascist propaganda also caricatured black women in their colonies as sexually available prizes of conquest...

...and later, with the Allied invasion of Southern Europe in 1943, the sexually threatening Black GI as rapist. The opulent, decadent Anglo-American was another Italian image.

Symbols and Rituals

The swastika, from the Sanskrit word **svasti**, "well being", an ancient sun symbol. Symbol of the "pure" Germans descended from a mythical Aryan folk.

One of Fascism's many symbols.

And its many rituals...

- participation in mass rallies and ceremonials
- swearing public oaths of loyalty kissing the national flag
- the Fascist cult of death
- at roll-calls it was customary to answer "present" after the names of dead comrades

Architecture

Fascist state architecture was grandiose and classical, looking back to the splendours of Imperial Rome.

The EUR 42 complex of buildings outside Rome was planned as the site for a great Universal Roman Exhibition **(Esposizione Universale Romana)** in 1942.

Italian architecture, as in literature and the arts, differed from Germany in being influenced by Futurist modernism which took at its face value Fascism's claim to be "revolutionary". The result was a style that ran contrary to pompous "imperial" architecture and produced some excellent building and urban planning.

The End of Fascism?

High ranking German officers were involved in a plot to overthrow Hitler in 1944 when it became clear that the war was certain to be lost.

German Fascism was defeated not by internal opposition, but by external force of arms - chiefly by the Red Army which sustained enormous losses in its advance from Stalingrad to Berlin.

Japan's brand of Fascism was also defeated by superior Allied forces.

Spain's Fascism dwindled away under post- war social and economic forces - chiefly under pressure from the United States and the NATO alliance which desired a secure Mediterranean in the Cold War era.

The case of Italy is different - as we shall see later.

The Allied victory saw the end of certain typical **kinds** and **styles** of Fascism. There is no reason to suppose that other kinds of Fascism might not emerge with different and possibly less easily identifiable styles.

Believing that the Allied victory "ended Fascism" depends on accepting that such a victory really did change the economic, and social structures of the ex-Fascist countries and their collaborators. Did this change really take place?

Let's look at Japan after its Unconditional Surrender in 1945.

The Reverse Course and the Cold War

WE HAVE A NAME FOR WHAT REALLY HAPPENED IN THE FIRST YEARS OF THE U.S. OCCUPATION OF JAPAN- <u>GYAKU KOSU.</u>

IT MEANS THE "REVERSE COURSE" IN U.S. POLICY.

The most important "change" in the post-war era was the Cold War, chiefly directed by the American government and its agencies against the Soviet Eastern bloc.

US Secretary of State James Byrnes expressed the real aims of American post-war foreign policy most bluntly.

WHAT WE HAVE TO DO NOW IS NOT MAKE THE WORLD SAFE FOR DEMOCRACY, BUT TO MAKE IT SAFE FOR THE UNITED STATES.

How did the "reverse course" relate to "making the world safe for the United States"?

In 1945, the Allies and the New Deal Democrats in Washington had aimed at two major democratic reforms of Japan.

1. To root out all Fascist elements in every department of government, the military, finance and industry.

2. To dismantle the giant **zaibatsu** monopolies in finance and industry which had been implicated in Japan's war machine and create a genuinely democratic free enterprise economy.

Were these reforms fulfilled?

Japan's Last Shogun

General Douglas MacArthur, as Supreme Commander of the US Occupation forces in Japan till 1951, had virtually autonomous powers of decision-making.

There was little effective "purge" of Fascist elements in the bureaucracy, politics and big business.

Rather than liquidate the proscribed right-wing organizations, G-2 Section military intelligence employed them to investigate Communist activities.

The giant cartels - Nissan, Mitsubishi, Toshiba, etc. - were not dismantled but supported by US big business investment.

The Cold War soon developed into a nasty little hot war in Korea (1950) which brought Red China into the conflict. The war on Communism also went on in the French colony of Indochina and the British one in Malaya - stages in the build up to Vietnam.

THE U.S. CONTRIBUTED MOST TO THE U.N. EXPEDITIONARY FORCES IN KOREA.

NOT THE FIRST TIME AMERICA HAS USED THE U.N. AS A COVER FOR PROMOTING ITS OWN INTERESTS!

This explains Japan's "Economic Miracle" of recovery.

The Armed Forces That Don't Exist

Japan's armed forces - named the **jieitai** or Self-Defence Forces - count among the world's largest and most efficient. But the SDF isn't supposed to exist. According to Article 9 of the Occupation-imposed Peace Constitution:

On 25 November 1970, the writer and Nobel Prize condidate, Yukio Mishima, with three members of his private paramilitary cadet force, kidnapped a general at sword-point in a Tokyo military headquarters.

Article 9

...the Japanese people forever renounce war as a sovereign right of the nation...land, sea, and air forces, as well as other war potential, **will never be maintained.** The right of belligerency of the state will not be recognized.

I DEMAND TO ADDRESS THE ENTIRE PERSONNEL OF THE HQ!

Mishima's speech was a call to overturn the Peace Constitution and restore the Emperor to power by a military coup. He pointed out the glaring contradiction of an illegal "shadow army".

THE SDF PROTECTS
THE VERY INSTITUTION
WHICH DENIES
ITS RIGHT TO EXIST -
THE PEACE CONSTITUTION!

Mishima failed to incite a military rebellion. In the general's office, he committed ritual **seppuku** (hara-kiri). Many questions about Mishima's act of terrorism have never been answered - in particular, how did he as a private citizen gain official permission to train his illegal force of paramilitary cadets jointly with the SDF? Right-wing paramilitary societies were not uncommon in his day, but they have become more noticeable since as bodyguards of right-wing politicians in league with the Mafia-style **yakuza** underworld.

On 16 October 1992, the **International Herald Tribune** reported SDF Major Shinsaku Yanai's call for a military coup "to cleanse Japan of corruption".

And in Occupied Germany?

Although the purge of Nazi officials in the Allied zones of Occupation was initially more effective (2.5% of the German population affected in the US sector alone, as opposed to 0.29% in all of Japan), it soon came to a halt. Again, as in Japan, the programme of dismantling the huge industrial monopolies went into reverse and West Germany was quickly rebuilt as an American ally in the Cold War.

IN PURSUIT OF OUR ANTI-SOVIET POLICY, WE'RE PREPARED TO OVERLOOK THE WAR CRIMES OF SOME FORMER NAZIS.

German scientists who invented the V-rockets used to bomb London were recruited to help NASA develop American rocketry.

Intelligence agencies set up by the Nazis were taken over.

In March 1964, Heinrich Lübke, the President of the Federal German Republic, awarded the industrialist Heinrich Bütefisch with the **Grosses Bundesverdienstkreuz,** the highest civilian honour. Lübke had designed concentration camps and organized slave labour for the production of V-rockets. Bütefisch had been convicted at the Nuremberg Trials for his part in IG Farben's special camp at Auschwitz - an extermination camp managed by the SS in partnership with Europe's (then) largest industrial corporation.

Siemens made an agreement with the SS to get cheap labour in Auschwitz, Buchenwald and Ravensbruck. BMW drew its slave labour from Dachau, IG Farben built its own concentration camp next to Auschwitz. IG Auschwitz (as it was called by the directors) was designed to produce artificial rubber. At least 50,000 inmates died building the factory.

IG Auschwitz was the company's biggest investment costing 250 million dollars at 1941 prices.

And What About Former Collaborators?

Let's take an example from Vichy France.

In 1942, Maurice Papon was secretary-general to the prefecture of the department of the Gironde with its capital in Bordeaux. He was responsible for the deportation of 1,690 Jews from the area. In 1961 he was Chief of Police in Paris when some 200 peaceful Algerian demonstrators were killed. In 1981 he was Minister for the Budget in the government of Giscard d'Estaing.

Papon is not a single isolated case of an unpurged former Vichy collaborator.There are hundreds more like him, both major and minor war criminals, left unprosecuted.

Shelter and Escape Routes

In the immediate post-war years, large numbers of Fascists who had survived military defeat and the collapse of the totalitarian regimes were still at large and frequently still in positions of authority.

Initially, much Fascist activity was confined to saving and sheltering important figures in the old Fascist organizations and forming links across frontiers.

Franco's Spain, Salazar's Portugal and various South American countries were safe havens for fugitive Fascists. Italy also offered escape routes with Vatican connivance. In the Vichy part of France once governed by Pétain, the Church sheltered Nazi war criminals.

The Case of Italy

The defeat of Fascism in Italy took a unique course. On 10 July 1943, Anglo-American forces landed in Sicily - materially assisted by the Mafia. In July 1943, King Victor Emmanuel dismissed Mussolini from office.

Marshal Badoglio, a right-wing Monarchist, made an Armistice deal with the Allies in Southern Italy and joined them in the war against Nazi Germany.
In the North, under German occupation, Mussolini set up the Salò Republic puppet government.

The armed struggle of the Italian Resistance in the North was directed both against Salò Republican forces and the German army.
Winston Churchill was determined to undermine the social and political demands of the Resistance.

King Victor Emmanuel, tainted by association with Mussolini, abdicated in favour of his son Umberto. Popular disgust with the monarchy was shown in the 1947 referendum when Italy opted for a republic.

BUT THERE WAS OTHERWISE NO CLEAN BREAK WITH THE PAST.

Abyssinians, Greeks and Yugoslavs had lists of war criminals, including Badoglio and other high ranking officers.

BUT THE BRITISH BLOCKED ANY ATTEMPTS TO BRING THEM TO JUSTICE.

The Allies' desire to achieve a smooth Cold War transition to the new democracy meant that Fascist laws remained on the statute books, and Fascist judges and officials remained in place. The Fascist prefects (the central government's provincial representatives) remained in power, as did the Fascist heads of the police.

Although Britain was the dominant power in the last stages of the war in Italy, in peace time the US emerged as the supporter of the democratic Right, subsidizing right-wing trade unions, injecting money and propaganda at election times, determined to block the Left .

American fears of a possible Communist electoral victory in 1948 because of its leading role in the Resistance led to large-scale interventions by the US government and its secret services. Notorious Fascists were recruited, financed and armed for the stay-behind underground organization **Gladio** (The Sword) set up for use against the Left and the imagined threat of a Soviet invasion of Western Europe. These elements formed dangerous alliances with branches of the CIA-backed Italian secret services and the military.

Consequences of the Cold War Policy in Italy

A state of unresolved tension between the Left, Right and the centre democrats helps to explain what subsequently happened in Italy.

In this political climate, the first neo-Fascist party quickly emerged. Called the **Fronte dell'Uomo Qualunque (The Common Man's Front),** it was financed by local bosses in the South and by ex-Fascists.

The Massacre of Communists in Sicily

Despite intimidation by the Church, the feudal landowners and their Mafia gunmen, Sicilian peasants voted against the Christian Democrats and in favour of Communist-inspired land reform on 20 April 1947.

The landowners and Mafia turned to Salvatore Giuliano for help. Giuliano, at 23 the "King of bandits", had begun his career as a Robin Hood dreamer of Sicilian separatist independence.

On orders from the Mafia barons, Giuliano's band machine-gunned a 1947 May Day rally at Portella della Ginestra, killing 11 people and wounding 55.

THEY WANT LAND? WE'LL GIVE IT TO THEM — SIX FOOT DEEP!

Giuliano's massacre plans were known to the police, Christian Democrat bosses and Allied Intelligence agencies.

The membership of the **Fronte** was soon absorbed by the Christian Democrat right wing and by the first significant neo-Fascist party in Western Europe, the MSI (Movimento Sociale Italiano). Like the **Fronte,** the MSI emerged in the South which had experienced neither a long German Occupation nor the Resistance.

In the 70s, neo-Fascism became a real threat to the democratic republic born of the Resistance.

The 70s were a time of severe economic recession in Italy. The right-wing Christian Democrats and the Communist Party were in a stalemate balance of power - the ideal climate of tension for the scenario of terrorism that would now unfold.

The Accidental Death of an Anarchist

In December 1969 a bomb exploded in a Milan bank, killing 16 people and wounding 88.

Two days later, Pinelli "fell" from the fourth floor office window of the police commissioner investigating the case.

WE ARRESTED A RAILWAYMAN - THE ANARCHIST PINO PINELLI - ON SUSPICION.

OBVIOUSLY SUICIDE.

It later emerged that those responsible for the bombing were neo-Fascists with links to the secret service (SID) and the MSI - by now a small but established party in parliament.

An Attempted Coup

In December 1970, Prince Julio Valerio Borghese, ex-commander of a notorious and murderous Salò Republican anti-partisan unit in 1944-45, occupied the Ministry of the Interior with former members of the parachute regiment led by an MSI politician. This attempted coup d'état was not revealed until March 1971, along with evidence of Borghese's membership in **Gladio,** his links with the army and the head of the secret service.

In 1974, four generals were accused of complicity All were acquitted.

The Black Eversion

Other neo-Fascist groups outside parliament, like the **Ordine Nuovo** (New Order - an MSI splinter group) and the **Nuclei Armati Rivoluzionari** (Armed Revolutionary Cells) were involved in terrorist attacks on members of the judiciary and bombed Bologna railway station in 1980, killing 86 people.

These and other terrorist atrocities at the time were blamed on extreme leftists, like the Red Brigade, in an effort to promote a "Red Scare". Red subversion was in fact orchestrated by the neo-Fascist "Black eversion" - all part of the continuing "strategy of tensions" by which the ultra-right hoped to create the preconditions for an authoritarian regime using the close links between the army, the secret services and the neo-Fascists.

Don't Ask Embarrassing Questions!

On 2 November 1975, the mangled corpse of the writer and film-maker Pier Paolo Pasolini was discovered on waste ground in Ostia, near Rome. The official verdict - that Pasolini was murdered in a homosexual encounter - remains in doubt. In the mid-70s, when kidnappings, assassinations and bombings were common, it is not impossible that some neo-Fascists decided to silence Pasolini, a notoriously outspoken "Commie fag".

I KNOW ALL ABOUT THE FASCIST PENAL CODE THAT IS STILL IN FORCE. IT HAS BEEN USED COUNTLESS TIMES IN CENSORSHIP AND OTHER PROSECUTIONS AGAINST ME.

Hardly a month before his murder, Pasolini asked these questions in a newspaper article (**Corriere della Sera**, 28 September 1975).

...over the whole of Italy's democratic life there looms the suspicion of Mafia-like complicity on the one hand, and of ignorance on the other; from this is born almost of its own accord a natural pact with power - a tacit diplomacy of silence.

The Italians want to know what the real role of Sifar*(1) was.

The Italians want to know what the real role of Sid* (2) was.

The Italians want to know what the real role of the CIA was.

The Italians want to know to what extent the Mafia took part in the decisions of the Rome Government or collaborated in it.

The Italians want to know what the reality of the so-called Fascist 'coups' was.

The Italians want to know in whose mind, and at what level, the idea of "the strategy of tensions" (first anti-Communist and then anti-Fascist, indiscrimately) was launched.

The Italians want to know who instigated and are materially responsible for the massacres in Milan, Brescia and Bologna.

But the Italians - and this is the heart of the matter - want to know all these things as a whole along with all the other potential crimes with which I began the list. Until they know all these things the political consciousness of the Italians will be incapable of producing a new awareness. That is to say Italy will not be governable.

*(1) Military intelligence (name now changed).
*(2) Counter intelligence service (now suppressed)

Asking these (and other) embarrassing
questions in 1975 would have
been enough to get
Pasolini
killed.

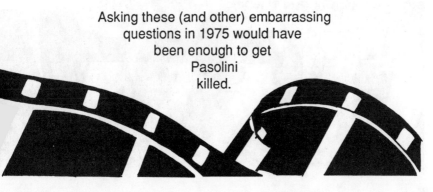

The MSI remains strong in the backward South of Italy. But in the richer, industrially advanced North, Fascist style "Leagues" began to appear in the 80s. Support for these "Leagues" comes partly from working class voters disillusioned with the Left.

THE LEFT HAS LET US DOWN.

OUR PARLIAMENTARY SYSTEM IS CORRUPT AND DOESN'T WORK.

WE'RE FED UP WITH THE POWER OF THE MAFIA...

AND THE ECONOMIC BURDEN OF CARRYING SOUTHERN ITALIANS.

The Leagues represent contempt for parliamentary government, and something new - racism. Racism has not traditionally been a factor in Italian political life. But now there is racism aimed at Southern Italians, Africans and Moroccans.

ITALIAN JOBS FOR ITALIAN WORKERS

EUROPE IS IN DANGER OF BEING ISLAMICIZED.

The Archbishop of Ravenna's warning against "Islamicization" uses a key term of the extreme Right in other countries.

The Case of Spain

Spain in the 70s saw a resurgence of Fascist violence. This was an expression of crisis as Franco's corporatist regime yielded to the demands of an expanding economy that required a more liberal political system - a movement leading to the return of the monarchy after Franco's death.

Catholic liberal and left-wing forces began to emerge, and even the conservative **Opus Dei** (see p.65) distanced itself from the old Falange.

Extreme right-wing groups reacted by targeting left-wing bookshops, liberal Catholic publications and clergymen.

The **Guerillas of Christ the King** composed of students

Commandos of the Anti-Marxist Struggle

Fuerza Nueva (New Force) a neo-Fascist political association

The **Spanish Nationalist Socialist Party** declared Hitler and Mussolini "defenders of European civilization"

CND

Extreme rightism was a nostalgic throwback to Franco's dictatorship.
The most influential Fascist organization still functioning is CEDADE (Spanish Circle of Friends of Europe), founded in 1965, one of the most active groups in Europe with extensive links in other countries.

Neo-Nazism in Germany

Hitler's defeat and the banning of Fascist parties delayed the emergence of extreme right forces. Their reappearance as a considerable political tendency began in 1964 with the foundation of the NPD (**Nationaldemokratische Partei Deutschlands** – National Democratic Party) formed by amalgamating a number of smaller groups. The NPD played on the resentments of refugees from the East and stressed the concept of the **Volk** – the mythical community of the German people.

The NDP today has strong links with the DVU (**Deutsche Volksunion** - German People's Union) which formed List D (for Deutschland) in the 1989 European elections, gaining nearly a half-million votes.

The leader of the alliance, Dr Gerhard Frey, is the owner of a press empire which pours out material aimed at revising Germany's wartime history and wiping out the **Kriegsschuldlüge** - the lie of war guilt.

More important is the REP (Republican Party) founded in 1983, whose leader Franz Schoenhuber is a former Waffen SS man. In 1989 the REP got over 2 million votes in the European Parliament elections and thereby won 6 seats in Strasbourg.

On the strength of a 7% showing in the national opinion polls and up to 10% of the vote in one German **Land,** the REP claims to be an established conservative party. It stands for a strong Germany, restoration of Germany's pre-WW2 frontiers, moral and spiritual renewal, and above all tighter controls over foreigners. It proposes typical Fascist policies - the subordination of trade unions to the state, compulsory training of girls for the role of wife and mother, censorship, and the withholding of social security and political rights from foreigners. The REP attempts to distance itself from violent extremists, but its rise to prominence has been accompanied by increased attacks on foreigners.

What about Neo-Nazi Violence?

Attacks on foreigners increased after the unification of Germany's (West) Federal and (East) Democratic Republics. In 1991, there were over 1,300 cases – a fivefold increase. 30% of these attacks took place in the former East Germany. Neo-Nazi skinheads armed with petrol bombs, chains and baseball bats frequently attack hostels, discotheques and camping sites.

This trend began in West Germany long before unification.
Militant neo-Fascist groups received military training, disposed of large caches of arms, and organized attacks on foreigners and on Jewish property.
Militants attacked a Munich Beer Festival in 1980, killing 12 people.

In the former East German DDR, racism has been directed at foreign workers - many of them Vietnamese.
Black workers and students, Poles and homosexuals are also objects of xenophobic hatred.

After the fall of the Berlin Wall, two hardline neo-Nazi formations emerged – **Deutsche Alternativen** (German Alternatives) and the **Freiheitliche Deutsche Arbeiterpartei** (Libertarian German Workers' Party).

The German authorities calculated that hardcore Fascist activists increased from 22,000 in 1989 to 40,000 in 1992. Of these, over 4,000 were officially described as "extremely violent skinheads".

Some Reasons for Neo-Nazism

What's behind the resurgence of Fascism in Germany? There are certain recognizable problems that trigger a Fascist reaction.

The Collapse of a Left Alternative

West Germany had an effective Left opposition in the Social Democratic Party (SPD). In the post-war period, the SPD's critical presence guaranteed that West German Conservatism would not develop into narrow right-wing Nationalism.

The SPD opposed rigid Cold War anti-Communism and instead promoted **Ostpolitik** - dialogue with the dictatorships of Eastern Europe, a precursor of **Glasnost** and **Perestroika**.

The SPD's reformism and moderation also inoculated the West German working class against the Cold War virus of Stalinist Communism.

A COLLAPSE OF THE ECONOMY IN THE EAST.

AND WIDESPREAD UNEMPLOYMENT.

These are conditions that encourage resentment at immigrants, foreign workers and political asylum-seekers - and there are plenty of them in the former Federal Republic.

BUT THE COLLAPSE OF COMMUNISM DEPRIVED THE SPD OF ITS ROLE AND IT BECAME IDENTIFIED WITH THE "APPEASEMENT OF COMMUNISM".

Where Does That Leave Germany's Conservatives?

The centre conservative force in West Germany has long been represented by the Christian Democrats. Christian Democratic leaders have constantly maintained that Germany is not "an immigration country" and have campaigned under the slogan "the boat is full" to restrict political asylum rights.

Immigrants have been treated as outsiders impossible to assimilate into German society. This has fostered a climate of hostility against foreigners which spilled over into neo-Nazi attacks.

Christian Democrats responded to the violence by making further concessions to the racists with promises of tighter controls on the "foreigner problem".

Neo-Fascism in Eastern Europe

Fascist movements quickly re-emerged after the collapse of the Soviet-dominated totalitarian regimes in Eastern Europe Skinhead groups using the Iron Cross have appeared in Hungary. In Slovakia, supporters of the Fascist priest, Tiso, who ruled there during the war, have surfaced.

In Russia, **Pamyat'**(Memory), a nationalist anti-Semitic organization has strong support, allied with **The People's Russian Orthodox Movement** which is monarchist and anti-Semitic.

The Russian Freedom Movement has revived the swastika.

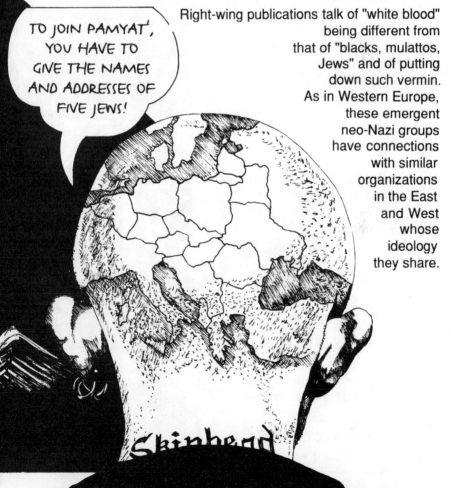

TO JOIN PAMYAT', YOU HAVE TO GIVE THE NAMES AND ADDRESSES OF FIVE JEWS!

Right-wing publications talk of "white blood" being different from that of "blacks, mulattos, Jews" and of putting down such vermin. As in Western Europe, these emergent neo-Nazi groups have connections with similar organizations in the East and West whose ideology they share.

Neo-Fascism in Britain

Racism is no less active in Britain than in Germany (and elsewhere). Something like 70,000 racial incidents occur every year in Britain, ranging from "minor" harassments to fire-bombings.

Neo-Fascist groups began by making a target of the black immigrants arriving from the Caribbean in the 50s.

STRICTER CONTROL OVER IMMIGRATION

Transport and General Workers Union (TGWU)
at its 1955 conference.

1958 brought the Nottingham and Notting Hill race riots.

The 60s and 70s saw the exodus to Britain of many Asians expelled from newly independent African nations.

AS COMMONWEALTH CITIZENS, WE HAVE A RIGHT TO ENTER BRITAIN.

NOT NOW - WITH RISING UNEMPLOYMENT AND CUTS IN WELFARE!

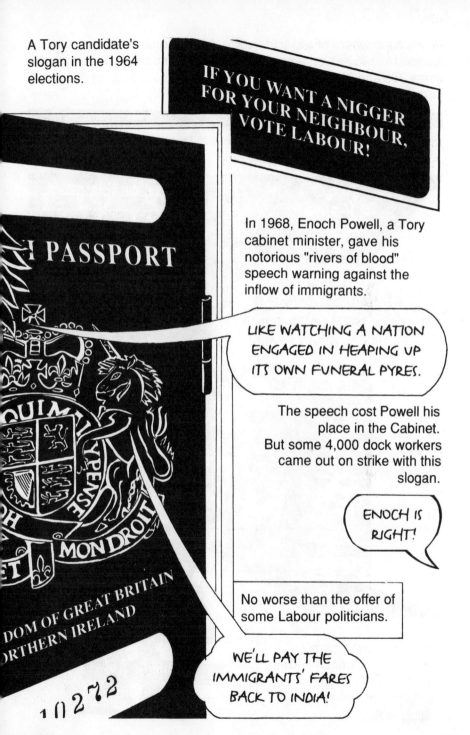

A Tory candidate's slogan in the 1964 elections.

IF YOU WANT A NIGGER FOR YOUR NEIGHBOUR, VOTE LABOUR!

PASSPORT

In 1968, Enoch Powell, a Tory cabinet minister, gave his notorious "rivers of blood" speech warning against the inflow of immigrants.

LIKE WATCHING A NATION ENGAGED IN HEAPING UP ITS OWN FUNERAL PYRES.

The speech cost Powell his place in the Cabinet. But some 4,000 dock workers came out on strike with this slogan.

ENOCH IS RIGHT!

No worse than the offer of some Labour politicians.

WE'LL PAY THE IMMIGRANTS' FARES BACK TO INDIA!

In this atmosphere of racial prejudice, the **National Front** was founded in 1967 as an amalgamation of extreme right splinter groups. In the 70s and 80s, the NF established itself as the leading Fascist party in Britain. Where did it get its membership?

In 1976, the NF polled 46% of the vote in Lewisham, a South London district with a large black population.

THERE WAS DISILLUSIONMENT WITH LABOUR IN LOCAL GOVERNMENT.

And votes came as in pre-war times from the lower middle class, manual workers and unemployed young males.

In 1977, the NF planned a march through Lewisham.

WE ASKED THE HOME OFFICE TO BAN IT.

NO! THIS IS A QUESTION OF FREE SPEECH.

The Lewisham Council

As in the 1936 Cable Street battle the Fascists were met by a counter demonstration organized this time not by the communist party but by the Socialist Workers' Party supported by black youths and individual members of the Labour and Communist Parties.

Merlyn Rees, Labour Home Secretary.

The High Court also refused.

The Fascist march had to disperse under police protection. Then the police attacked the anti-Fascist demonstrators, making over 200 arrests.

The National Front made great efforts to establish itself in the unions and had members in the railway and at the Leylands car factory.

The NF found the Industrial Relations Act of 1971 (one of the Tory government's first steps to control the unions) too **weak!**

The National Front was subject to leadership splits and rivalries. In the early 80s the British Movement emerged. It has a cell-structured secret group called the **British Nationalist Socialist Movement** with very strong links abroad. In 1982 the British National Party was founded and has since become the most important of the extreme right-wing groupings. It is an openly Nazi party whose leading figures have serious criminal convictions, ranging from bomb-making to the organization of illegal paramilitary groups, the possession of firearms and offences under the Race Relations and Public Order Acts. There are also a number of small groups some of which have engaged in arms trafficking. A very influential body is the **League of St George** founded in 1974. It has only 50 members who are mainly very wealthy. It has sheltered German Fascists accused of involvement in terrorist activities in Italy.

A Left Opposition to the NF

In 1977, the Anti-Nazi League took shape from a united front of SWP and left-wing Labour MPs. The ANL's support among unions and local Labour Parties, and its alliance with **Rock against Racism** which won the enthusiasm of many young people, led to the NF's collapse at subsequent local elections.

In the new century, the number of people seeking refuge in Britain has been greatly increased by war in the Balkans, by racism directed against minorities like gypsies, and by economic deprivation. The treatment of these refugees has become a political issue. In some reception areas in the south of England, refugees have become the targets of racism. In what has been seen as the run-up to a General Election, which must take place by 2004, the issue has been debated in language that is often intemperate. There is a feeling that the Labour Party is fearful of being seen as "soft" on the subject; the Conservatives have been accused of exploiting grassroots prejudices – in fact, of "stealing the thunder" of right-wing extremists.

WHAT HAPPENS IF THE ELECTORATE LOSES PATIENCE WITH THE CONSERVATIVE "FIX"?

AND THERE'S NO CONFIDENCE IN THE LEFT....

SAME POTENTIAL RISK AS WE'VE SEEN IN ITALY AND GERMANY!

Neo-Fascism in France

The rise of an extreme right became apparent in the 60s when Africans, Algerians and Jews came under racist attacks.

Small terrorist groups emerged with names like **Youth Front, Christian West, Delta Commandos.** Their attacks on persons and shops peaked in the 80s with over 60 such "actions".
235 specifically anti-Semitic incidents were also recorded.

The **Front National** (FN) led by
Jean-Marie Le Pen is a more
important political formation.
Set up in 1972, the FN
now claims 100,000 members
and 200,000 sympathizers.

Support for the FN Party reflects the
pattern of other Fascist formations.

1. An overwhelmingly middle and
   lower middle class membership.

2. Working class voters disillusioned
   with the Left, in particular the
   Communist Party.

3. Typically again, the FN promotes
   itself as voicing the workers'
   concerns by defending them from
   Capitalism on the one hand and
   the Reds on the other.

The FN is well represented at local levels.
Significantly, it has influence in the judiciary, the armed forces and the police.
It has marginalized and absorbed smaller right wing groups (but which have not ceased all activity).

The NF is particularly strong in Marseilles and Perpignan in the south of France where it takes 30% of the vote. This is a region which has many white ex-colonists, the **pieds noirs** (black feet), who chose to return from Algeria after the country's independence from France in 1962.

Traditional right-wing conservative parties in the south have also entered into informal electoral pacts with the FN.

The rise of the FN coincides with racism directed at the 4 million or so immigrants. 3 million of these come from the Maghreb in North Africa, some of whom - the Harkis - collaborated with the French forces in Algeria.
This outbreak of racism is partly fed by memories of the long and bloody colonial war in Algeria.*
But another reason is the arrival on the labour market of second generation immigrants at a time of recession and unemployment.

*In Paris on October 21 1961, 200 Algerians taking part in a peaceful demonstration against police restrictions were murdered by the police and their bodies dumped in the Seine.

Children of immigrants are seen as aggravating a crisis in the educational system.
There is widespread apprehension at a perceived threat of the "Islamicization" of French culture .

Prejudice and violence against immigrants is accompanied by anti-Semitic attacks and the desecration of Jewish cemeteries. One such desecration in 1990 resulted in a huge protest march in Paris led by the President of the Republic, François Mitterand.

The FN is typically Fascist in its condemnation of homosexuality and abortion, its appeal to national pride and "family values", and its talk of the "the national priority" of the French people - of whom ironically one in three is descended from immigrants to France in the first hundred years.

In 1984 the FN won 10 seats in the European Parliament. In 1986 it secured 35 seats in the French National Assembly. In the 1988 presidential elections the FN won over 14% of the vote.

The Spread of Neo-Fascism

On a smaller scale, similar manifestations of Fascist thought and activity are to be found in Austria, in Belgium and The Netherlands, in Denmark, Sweden and Norway.

What they have in common is the rise of parties which gain representation at a local or national level on a platform of racist and anti-Semitic policies. Examples are the Austrian Freedom Party (FPO), the Centre Democrats (CD) in Holland, the Vlaams Blok (Flemish Block) and the Front National in Belgium.

Alongside these legal parties there are neo-Nazi groups which employ direct - action bomb attacks on Jewish cemeteries in Austria, bomb attacks on immigrants and asylum-seekers. In Denmark, the National Socialist League advocates a purge of immigrants, the death sentence on anyone passing on AIDS and compulsory sterilization of non-white adopted children. These neo-Nazi formations have links across Europe with similar organizations in Germany, France, Spain, Britain. Nor should we overlook the international links with ultra-nationalist and neo-Nazi groups in the United States.

Did Hitler Really Exist?

THIS MYTH OF THE MASS MURDER OF JEWS IN THE DEATH FACTORIES OF AUSCHWITZ.....
....WHICH IN FACT NEVER TOOK PLACE.

David Irving

No sane person would dispute the existence of Hitler. Countless eye witness reports, photos and massive documentation put Hitler's reality beyond doubt.

And yet, there are neo-Fascists who would deny the fact of the Holocaust which is based on precisely the same kind of overwhelming evidence - eye witnesses, photos and detailed documentation. Prominent among the academics engaged on this "revision" of history - trying to prove that the Holocaust either did not take place or has been wildly exaggerated - are Professor Paul Rassinier in France and British historian David Irving who describes himself as a "mild Fascist".

What is the point of "disproving" the Holocaust? The aim is to minimize the staggering evils of Nazism and if possible acquit Hitler himself of any crimes against humanity. The aim is to replace the real Hitler with the myth of an acceptable leader.

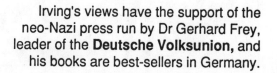

Neo-Fascism is seeking to make itself **respectable**.

Irving's views have the support of the neo-Nazi press run by Dr Gerhard Frey, leader of the **Deutsche Volksunion,** and his books are best-sellers in Germany.

The Respectable Right

It is dangerously misleading to think of the Far Right simply in terms of neo-Nazi skinhead hooligans. More important and more powerful supporters of neo-Fascism can be found in "respectable society" - in the judiciary, police, the military, finance and industry. Respectability is also the aim of the academic and intellectual "New Right".

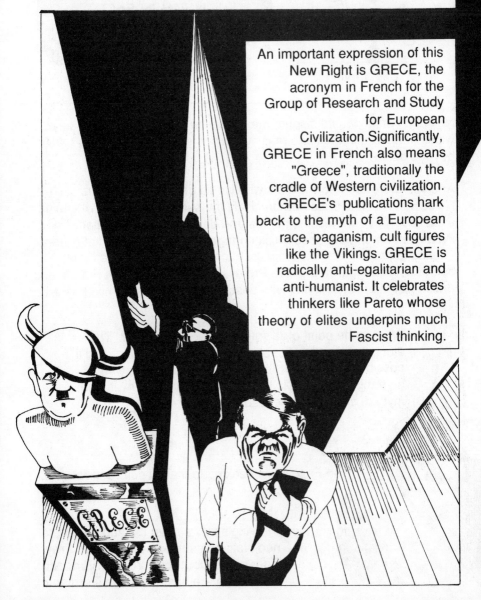

An important expression of this New Right is GRECE, the acronym in French for the Group of Research and Study for European Civilization.Significantly, GRECE in French also means "Greece", traditionally the cradle of Western civilization. GRECE's publications hark back to the myth of a European race, paganism, cult figures like the Vikings. GRECE is radically anti-egalitarian and anti-humanist. It celebrates thinkers like Pareto whose theory of elites underpins much Fascist thinking.

The intellectual New Right is active not only in France, but in Italy, Germany, Britain and elsewhere.

This anti-egalitarian movement has adopted social biology, genetics and ethology to apply concepts of animal behaviour, such as "the pack" and "the dominant male", to human society.

New Right apologists peddle "scientific" theories about the inheritance of intelligence and its links with race.

An article in the medical journal The **Lancet** in 1972 suggested that the "increased prevalence of mental retardation" called for "urgent action". Such views are linked to the concept of "mental hygiene" and eugenic medicine.

In Britain, a leading proponent of this line of thought was Sir Cyril Burt (1883-1971). His work on the IQ of twins, aimed at discounting the importance of culture in the development of intelligence, is today discredited. He was a member of the Eugenics Society and a founder of MENSA, the high IQ group which believes in eugenic principles.

Neo-Fascism - "News Today, Gone Tomorrow?"

Should we be talking of the **resurgence** of Fascism, or its **continuity,** or a new and unknown variety of Fascism? Is neo-Fascism really "old wine in new bottles"?

We have given examples of neo-Fascist formations that have mushroomed in and since the Cold War era. Do all these - and more - add up to a single **unitary** threat of Fascism?

There have also been different right-wing tyrannies outside Europe in the last 50 years. Some examples are the apartheid regime in South Africa, Indonesia under Suharto, Haiti under "Papa Doc" Duval,Uganda under Idi Amin, Nicaragua under Somoza, Iran under the Shah and the Ayatollah Khomeni, Iraq under Saddam Hussein. Tyrannies they certainly were or are. But are they, properly speaking, **Fascist** regimes?

The social, economic and political conditions sustaining these (re) appearances of Fascism are fluid. Neo-Fascist groups or parties that have made the headlines in the 80s might indeed be "news today and gone tomorrow". We have to look beyond these phenomena to the underlying **persistent** conditions that could support Fascism in the long term.

1. Industrially advanced economies hard hit by the recessionary slump.

2. A discredited Left alternative.

3. Dissatisfaction with an inefficient or corrupt parliamentary system.

4. An end of consensus politics.

5. Racism provoked by "job stealing" immigrants, refugees and political asylum-seekers.

6. A respectable Right.

7. Nostalgia for a strong state. This last calls for separate attention.

Nostalgia and Maladjustment

Nostalgia for a strong state involves the **psychological** dimensions of a nationalist "siege mentality".

1. A feeling of loss of identity or national prestige (for example, Britain's loss of empire) compensated for by jingoism and hooligan behaviour.

2. Difficulty of adjusting to a society in which large numbers of citizens are unemployed and unlikely ever to be employed - thanks to governments' economic reliance on "the market" which deepens the gap between rich and poor and results in the creation of a "sub-class", the euphemism for people the market has junked.

3. Inability to admit and come to terms with the realities today of multi-ethnic societies and cultures.

4. Blindness to a world facing an immense movement of populations as the poor and deprived leave countries where deserts are expanding, famine is endemic and life is intolerable.
The 19th century poor of Europe
emigrated to America and the British Empire.
The new wave of emigration
will be from the misery of Africa and Asia.
European govenments are
responding to this by tightening
immigration legislation and
denying asylum to
political refugees.

Finally...

How do we recognize whether a group, party or government qualifies as Fascist or not? One way of attempting a definition might be to tick off the headings in the following list:

Are their prime targets:
- ☐ trade unions?
- ☐ the Left?
- ☐ parliamentary democracy?
- ☐ are they supported by the middle classes?
- ☐ by disillusioned workers?
- ☐ do they appeal to youth?
- ☐ rely on support of military and police?
- ☐ are they racist?
- ☐ extreme nationalists?
- ☐ corporative?
- ☐ funded by industry or landowners?
- ☐ do they attempt to limit the role of women?
- ☐ are they hostile to homosexuality?
- ☐ do they oppose abortion?
- ☐ rely on a mass party?
- ☐ appeal to mythical history?
- ☐ use terrorism against opponents?
- ☐ enjoy the complicity of the authorities?
- ☐ exalt the Leader?

What's to be Done?

We should recall Hitler's own words in 1933.

"Only one thing could have stopped our movement – if our adversaries had understood its principle and from the first day had smashed with the utmost brutality the nucleus of our new movement."

Then, how do you answer the question?

☐ Do you share the view taken by most established political parties that the law is sufficient to deal with Fascism?

☐ Do you think the mobilization of Fascism's opponents and possible confrontation is the only tactic the Fascists respect?

You should tick the appropriate box.

Fascism – An Update

That demonstrations in the streets against Fascist tendencies can work was demonstrated in Austria, where early in the year 2000 the participation of the extreme nationalist Freedom Party in a right-wing coalition government led to large public protests. The Freedom Party was led by Jörg Haider, who has a record of nostalgia for Hitler, combined with xenophobia. The demonstrations led Haider to resign from his post as party leader, and to the insistence by the head of the Austrian state that the parties in the coalition should pledge themselves to respect human rights. Meanwhile, the European Union showed its disapproval by breaking off contacts with Austria, even though it is a member of the Union. The rise of the Freedom Party under Haider's leadership was seen as a warning to the rest of Western Europe.

Haider's career – his rise from a Nazi family background to become governor of the province of Carinthia – has to be seen against the post-war political history of Austria. The Allies who occupied it in 1945 made no attempt to carry out the kind of deNazification programme which (however limited, however lacking in thoroughness) was applied to Germany. Instead, they accepted the myth that Austria was not a partner in Hitler's Third Reich but a victim of Nazism. But film of Hitler's entry into Vienna after the Anschluss (the annexation of Austria) in 1938 shows him being greeted by huge and ecstatic crowds. Pictures of Viennese Jews being humiliated and forced to scrub the streets surrounded by jeering onlookers confirm a vicious anti-Semitism. The names of the concentration camps in Germany are well known. Less has been heard of Mauthausen in Austria, where there was a concentration camp notorious for its cruelty. Its inmates included Spanish Republican soldiers, Italian partisans, Italian strikers and political prisoners. Austria as a society was allowed to indulge in amnesia where its Nazi past was concerned. A notorious example was that of Kurt Waldheim, who when standing as candidate for the presidency of the country in 1986 lied about his involvement in Nazi war crimes in the Balkans, where he served as an officer.

This is the political background against which Haider rose to power and found support for his Freedom Party. In 1991, he claimed in the Austrian parliament that Hitler had at least pursued a 'competent employment policy' – which, he should have added, combined conscripted labour and a rearmament drive. He addressed war veterans including ex-members of the Waffen SS, and described them as 'decent people'. They were, he claimed, 'models for the youth of our time'. In his political statements he encouraged xenophobia directed against refugees and immigrants from the Balkans and Eastern Europe. He has declared it his intention to reduce the number of immigrant children in the classrooms of Austria. What rightly alarmed the demonstrators in Vienna was the fact that his party had become the second largest in Austria. Although in the face of popular dissent Haider resigned from the leadership of the party, this was read as a tactical move. He was still governor of Carinthia, and there was no doubt that he would continue to play a leading role in the party's policies. His stated aim is to become head of the Austrian state.

He found friends in Italy, where right-wing separatist politicians expressed their agreement with his policies. In Northern Italy – particularly in the province of Venezia Giulia, which is today the most flourishing part of the Italian economy – there is widespread and open racism. It is directed against what are described as 'extra-communitarians'. These include not only people of African origins and Romas (gypsies), accused of large-scale criminality, but also immigrants from Eastern Europe, Albania and the former Yugoslavia. In Treviso, the mayor did away with public seating in the main square because he disliked seeing blacks sitting there. In a country where under Mussolini racist policies found little support, this dangerous xeno-phobia has been gaining ground. The paradox is that in Italy, which has a very low rate of population growth, Venezia Giulia, the home of Benetton, would not be so prosperous without the help of the immigrants, legal and illegal, who do work that Italians are not prepared to undertake.

There are parallels to this xenophobia elsewhere in Europe. In Southern Spain, attacks on immigrants from North Africa have led to racial riots, even though the rural industry in which they work would suffer greatly if their labour were not available. In Britain, the language used by the local press in Dover when writing about immigrants has shown that racism is not some-thing foreign to the United Kingdom.

The movement of men and women from underprivileged parts of Africa and Europe to the more affluent West will continue. The problem is that unlike the United States in the days of its great wave of immigration, Europe has no 'empty territory'. (Neither did the USA – it was simply that the native Americans were swept aside.) The immigrants will compete for (low-paid) jobs and for social assistance. In Western Europe, the economic system has created a sub-class of disadvantaged citizens – many of them unemployed men. There is a pool of resentment that could be exploited by racist politi-cians. Should there be an economic recession, there is a danger that they could harness to their ends the violence and jingoism of the football crowds and the readiness of vigilantes to take the law into their own hands.

There is unmistakable evidence that in many parts of Europe – including Britain – racism is widespread. It is on racist fears the Fascism has built its following in the past. We are not necessarily on the edge of a Fascist resur-gence, but we have every reason to be on the alert against it.

Suggested Further Reading

Introductions

The following provide good background on the origins and rise of Fascism.
Hannah Arendt, **Origins of Totalitarianism**(London 1958). James Joll, **Europe since 1870** (London 1990 4th edition). S.J. Wolf (ed.), **Fascism in Europe** (London 1981).

General discussions of the post-war emergence of neo-Fascism can be found in: Cheles, Ferguson, Wright (eds.), **Neo-Fascism in Europe** (London 1991).

R. Thurlow, **Fascism in Britain** (London 1986), a history to the present.
Interesting but more difficult essays on the crisis developing in West Germany in the 1970s, J. Habermas (ed.) **Observations on "The Spiritual Situation of the Age"** (MIT Press 1987).

The Past History of Fascism

Italy

C.F. Delzell, **Mussolini's Enemies: The Anti-Fascist Movement** (Princeton 1961).

Paul Ginsborg, **A History of Contemporary Italy** (London 1990).

Gaetano Salvemini, **Prelude to World War II** (London 1953).

Elizabeth Wiskemann, **Europe of the Dictators** and **The Rome-Berlin Axis** (London 1966).

For the rise of neo-Fascism, consult Baranski and Lumley, **Culture and Conflict in Post War Italy** (London 1990).

Germany

The classic account is William L. Shirer's massive **The Rise and Fall of the Third Reich** (New York 1960-61).

A.J.P. Taylor, **The Origins of the Second World War** (London 1961) is provocative and controversial.

D. Peukert, **Inside Nazi Germany** (London 1989) provides a good inside picture.

Spain

The two classic accounts are: Gerald Brennan, **The Spanish Labyrinth** (London 1960) and Hugh Thomas, **The Spanish Civil War** (London 1977).

Also useful: A. Lloyd, **Franco** (London 1970) and Paul Preston, **The Politics of Revenge - Fascism and the Military in 20th Century Spain** (London 1990).

Japan

For a brief general introduction, try: Robert Storry, **A History of Modern Japan** (Penguin 1987).

David Bergamini, **Japan's Imperial Conspiracy** (London 1971) is a long, fascinating and controversial investigation of the Emperor's key role as architect of Japanese military expansion.

Jon Halliday, **A Political History of Japanese Capitalism** (New York and London 1975), an illuminating social and economic study of Japan from the 19th century to World War II, the Occupation and economic recovery.

Ivan Morris, **Nationalism and the Right Wing in Japan** (Oxford University Press 1960), an important assessment of the Occupation and the resurgence of extreme rightwing organizations in post-war Japan.

The Holocaust

The literature on the Holocaust is vast. For a useful introduction to the history of anti-Semitism try E.H. Flannery, **The Anguish of the Jews** (New York and London 1965). Norman Cohn, **Warrant for Genocide** (Penguin 1970) traces the impact of the fake "Protocols of the Elders of Zion" on Nazi propaganda. Zygmunt Bauman, **Modernity and the Holocaust** (London 1989) is stimulating and highly recommended.

Stuart Hood
writer, novelist, translator, documentary film maker, ex- BBC executive, ex-professor in film at the Royal College of Art. Honorary member of ANPI (National Association of Italian Partisans), unrepentant socialist

Litza Jansz
illustrator, designer, animator, Independent film-maker producing and directing films for C4 and the BBC.
Lecturer in Media Studies and Animation.
unrepentant socialist.

---

with thanks to the **Imperial War Museum**, the **Wiener Library** and for the useful service provided by the local libraries of Camberwell.

A particular thanks to Norma for offering her expertise and support throughout the project.Thanks to Natty - an invaluable advisor.

Typesetting by Norma Spence

Index